A Christmas Trilogy

Mike Kelley

A Christmas Trilogy

A Christmas Trilogy
by
Mike Kelley

PUBLISHED by PARABLES
Earthly Stories with a Heavenly Meaning

Mike Kelley

———————————

A Christmas Trilogy
Mike Kelley

Published By Parables
November, 2019

All Rights Reserved. No part of this book may be reproduced or utilized in any form or by any means, electronic or mechanical, including photocopying, recording, or by any information storage and retrieval system, without permission in writing from the author.

    ISBN 978-1-951497-77-4
    Printed in the United States of America

Readers should be aware that Internet Web sites offered as citations and/or sources for further information may have been changed or disappeared between the time this was written and the time it is read.

A Christmas Trilogy

A Christmas Trilogy
By
Mike Kelley

PUBLISHED by PARABLES
Earthly Stories with a Heavenly Meaning

Mike Kelley

A Christmas Trilogy

DEDICATION

Dedicated to: My Grandmother long beyond this world, Florence Spain, to all my brothers, Donald, Carl, Dennis, and my most loving sister, Joy Spain Holder.

Mike Kelley

The works to follow are three very different Christmas stories. I have also sprinkled in a few Christmas poems. This I do with a prayer that you find in you, peace in happiness.

Welcome to a Christmas Trilogy.
Mike Kelley

A Christmas Trilogy

Table of Contents:

Greetings, A Christmas Wish

The Bus Driver's Last Christmas

If I could pull the ropes that ring the Bells of Christmas

A Christmas Ride

Will we be thinking of him?

Grandma's Bible

Noel

Christmas Greetings

Greetings to all:

Softness falls to the mind

Lifting like the glow from a candle

Old memories bring another smile

Christmas is at hand

Miles apart, yet together in hearts

Music floats in the air, lifting a spirit of joy

Cards and letters usher, wishes warmly

Welcome from a wreath upon the door

Recall those treats, homemade candies and cookies

A Christmas Trilogy

The joy to look out a frosted window, and see a Christmas snow

It is a time of magic, in ribbons and bows

And a kiss under the mistletoe

There is a place for that pine, and the fragrance it sends

The bells that ring, as church doors open to celebrate

The hand that fills yours, from a ghost of Christmas past

A Father, Mother, Grand Father or Grand Mother are there

Tears warm, in a loving recall may fall

Children with wide eyes, and toy dreams

There is a cold breeze from the North Pole

But there is also a star in Bethlehem

A child so holy, kings came to worship

The old Family Bible turns to the second chapter of Luke

A candle is to be lighted, and a prayer for us all

To those we love, to this world, and to his kingdom

Let the lights of Christmas shine

Let the bells ring

Let us celebrate

It is, a Merry Christmas wish

The Bus Drivers Last Christmas

A Christmas Trilogy

The bus driver's last Christmas

When driving a bus in a large city most drivers are hammered on by traffic, angry people always running late, folks that drink too much, and sometimes people of just an evil heart. Then sometimes there are people that stand out of the empty faces, those that become a distant family of sorts. This story is about one man in his last year driving, after twenty-four years on bus 7123.

Strange it would be at Christmas that would end his career with the City Bus Company, yet Johnny Deamer, was on his last 100 miles trip around the city in four 25, mile circuits. He had not taken vacation and had to take it before he retired to receive his final payout.

It was 5:15 AM as he clocked in for his 6AM run around town. He would leave the main terminal at 5:30AM and he was always a man on time even when the weather was bad. His record of safe driving had made him a standard, one other drivers tried to achieve.

It was a beautiful time to see the city with the colored lights in the stores, decorated trees, All the "Santa's" ringing bells, and to feel the joy of the season in the air. Today snow was falling and it was just the setting for some artist to paint, a City at Christmas.

Johnny however was feeling a bit lost as this was the end of the line for him with no future beyond his job, his eyes had seen it all through the years, but now they were framed in glasses, his beard that was once red now white, his hands with age spots. Tomorrow would be a day that the world would rejoice in the Christmas celebrations, but Johnny would sit with his dog Bozo and watch the snow fall, have a cup of warm cider and listen to the music from his radio in the small kitchen of his little house. He would attend the service at the local mission, then after would serve cake and coffee. He would stand with the homeless by a piano, one a bit out of tune, and sing the songs of the season, then help serve a Christmas meal before going home. This had been his celebration for the past many years now onto seventeen years since his wife passed. He would visit her stone on Christmas morning, always leaving a gift of flowers and a card.

Today, this morning he arrived at his first stop and the faces boarded one by one each inserting a token into the coin exchange and taking a seat. Today they arrived with their boxes and ribbons for giving. Smiles were the uniform of the day and this brighten the face of Johnny.

This would be the 6 to 8 run and then he would load again for the 8:30 to 10:30 run. Snow now was falling a little heavy on this his second run and this would slow him some as he always allowed a distance for the other drivers on the road to make changes in road conditions.

This was also his favorite run of the day as there were so many folks that daily rode, he had learned to know them through the years. They talked of everything openly with him, he knew whose children had issues, who had a job that was on the line, who had just had a new baby, and sadly who lost a love one to time.

Mr. Watson was the first to board and he had a new book in hand he would sit in the seat just behind Johnny and fill him in on the story and then the two would try to figure out what would happen in the next chapter, and laugh together when they missed. Watson must have thought he was like onto Dr. Watson with Mr. Homes, always it was a mystery to solve.

The bus was crowded this time as the road conditions put more on board in foul conditions. It was however, a joyful ride as several members of a glee club from the local High School were singing the songs of the season with many of the others joining in.

The third round was scheduled but there was an issue with a tire on the front of the bus that had gone flat and another bus and driver was dispatched on his third round as he had to await repairs to the bus to complete. This was his lunch stop so he opened his lunch box and took out a sandwich and coffee and sat eating and watching the snow. Inside the top of his lunch box was a picture of his wife, he would sit and talk to the picture as he had his lunch and tell her about the lovely falling snow.

Repairs made and this would be his last round for the day, and his last trip with the company. He would be picking up and bringing home those he called his family.

Leaving the terminal, he picked up the Chatty lady, she always had something to say about the news and the world, but in all his time driving he never knew her name, just her voice and opinions. She was followed by two young ladies that worked at the bank, they were like peas in a pod, both lovely and always happy and working in the world of money it was sad to see them count out their dimes for a ride home.

Larry Oaks was next to board he had dreams in music and was always carrying a case with his trumpet inside at the ready. Getting on at the same stop was Mimi a young lady that was a server at La Peeps Restaurant with her arms full of packages those for the special someone's in her life. And just behind her was Mrs. Cobb a lovely German woman who always had two shopping bags filled every time she was on the way home. She had reported she needed to have two to keep her from falling over to one side. She always had a silly little joke to tell, and she would be the only one that laughed at them, but she didn't care, she said it is in the telling that counts.

Snow was now filling a bit heavily the streets and crunching under the tires as they moved to the next stop where the preacher from a community church was on his way home after spending time with those in the local hospital. Then just before the door was to shut a man ran up yelling wait, and boarded at the last second. He hovered by the token and money exchange box a second and then pulled a gun from his worn jacket and told everyone to sit tight and not move.

Johnny was only a few feet from the man but unable to reach out to him from the driver's seat. Then the man told Johnny to drive on down the street and to not stop till he got to Elm.

People were in a panic with the Chatty lady screaming like someone was pulling her hair. The gunman told her to shut up or he would shoot her on the spot, but this only made her scream louder and without a thought longer he shot her in the shoulder and she passed out cold with the preacher standing to help and stop the blood flow the best he could. This the gunman allowed, but everyone on the bus now was in silence. There was no medical help on the bus, well except Mimi who was taking studies to become a nurse and she too was allowed to attend to the lady.

The preacher turned to the gunman and tried to talk him out of this action, but it was too late he had robbed a pawn shop and was on his way to leave the city with his cash.

Johnny passed the next stop without stopping, his riders stood and watched as the bus moved away. He was driving on ice the roads were frozen over and they were almost at elm when he skidded slightly, then the gunman told him to just keep on. In passing, the gunman cursed as he saw his car being towed away, he was parked in a zone for snow removal.

Things started to get out of control as the gunman told Johnny to take the on ramp to the expressway and drive north. Johnny told the gunman he had only enough fuel to drive 50 or so miles.

"Just drive" said the gunman, as he asked everyone on the bus to take out their cell phones and pass them to the front of the bus, and if anyone didn't, he would shoot them. It was a buzz of conversation, but the cell phones were passed forward and when he had them all he told Johnny to open the door and the phones were tossed out onto the snow and ice of highway.

Panic was setting in and Johnny was looking for a way to gain control as he was moving down the highway, he knew he couldn't brake fast on the ice, so the thought came about a rapid swerve taking an exit and knocking the gunman off his feet. It would be risky but, it might work. He watched for the next off ramp and then put the bus into a skid that slid it off the road into the exit. The bus tilted and he reached for the hand that held the gun but just as he almost got hold it went off and shot him.

Screams went up and the gunman took the gun again in hand and aimed it at the head of Johnny but instead of shooting him he came down on his head knocking him out cold. Johnny had been shot in the stomach area and was bleeding badly. The gunman tossed him to the floor of the bus and told the preacher to drive.

It was not an easy job to turn the bus around but the preacher got the bus off the ramp and back onto the freeway heading north. As the lady he had shot had now been bandaged and resting, Mimi asked the gunman if she could look after the bus driver. He grumbled out a few foul words and said for her to do what she could and to not try anything.

She looked around and then asked if she could have help getting him in a seat to stop the bleeding. Again, more foul words, and he pointed to Larry Oaks and told him to get up and drag the man to a seat. Larry quickly did when asked, and helped in the applying pressure to the wound to lessen the blood flow. This put him the closest person to the gunman and now his wheels were spinning in a way to gain control.

The preacher wasn't a good driver and on ice it was easy to see that he was going at a much slower pace just to keep the bus moving.

The gunman was trying to think what to do when he saw a flashing light coming up behind the bus and was ready to take on the law if needed. He stood beside the preacher and told him to keep on at a steady pace and just when he thought the bus was to be pulled aside the car went past heading towards another issue unaware of what this bus had going on.

Larry was whispering with Mimi, asking if she had anything in her bag, he might use to stop the gunman. "No, I don't think so" she said "but let me move around some things and see". She pulled out a scarf to use as a bandage and keep the gunman from thinking anything about it. Then Larry saw some fingernail polish remover and asked her for it thinking he might toss it in the eyes of the gunman long enough to take the gun away.

Just when he got his hands on it and was about to turn around, he was kicked in the head and then kicked again and again. Larry lay at the feet of Mimi out cold. Now Mimi had people all around her bleeding or out cold.

Then to make matters worse the gunman snatched her up by the hair and smacked her across the face and said, "I don't know if that stupid trick was your thinking or your boyfriends there, but just in case don't try anything again or it will be your blood next that will be flowing" then just for good measure he smacked her again.

Weather conditions worsen and the bus skidded off the road down into a wooded area and smashed into a tree. The preacher was laying across the steering wheel when he was shot in the back and didn't move. Those on the bus were tossed about, many with injuries.

"Damn fool" shouted the gunman, and he just put you folks in a bad way too" then he went from seat to seat and tied all the men's hands together with their belts and the women were secured by scarfs and purse straps. They were shoved like cattle to the back of the bus and told not to move or he would shoot at the pile of people and who ever dies, dies.

Mimi was the only one except for Larry and Johnny that wasn't tied up. The lady that was shot early on came around as the bus crashed, and she was sent with the other to the back of the bus with her hands tied together with shoestrings from the dead preacher's shoes.

People were crying and hurt in the crash of the bus, as the gunman took out a box of shells and reloaded his gun. "Anyone counting the bullets I fired can just forget it I have more shells then there are people on this bus",

The gunman opened the door with a gust of cold air rushing in and was going to leave them as they were, when a tree limb that was wedged over the top of the bus fell on him as the door opened. He was knocked to the ground as a section of the tree limb cut through his leg and now, he was wounded too.

Screaming he pulled the section of jagged limb from his leg; it had cut through his skin and he could see the bone in his right leg exposed. Pulling himself back in he called for Mimi to come to his aid. She looked at the injury and told him he would need to have hospital care to save his leg. His blood was spurting out at a rapid pace and she knew he would bleed out if something wasn't done fast. Quickly she took the belt from the dead preacher and put it around the leg and pulled it tight to slow the bleeding. She herself now covered in everyone's blood worked as best she could when she said that the cut end of the vessels needed sewed together and she had nothing to work with.

Johnny was coming around and heard the conversation and even as hurt as he was he told Mimi that there was a first-aid kit under the driver's seat and it might help, and in his bag beside the seat was a sewing kit he carried as he was always losing buttons.

Mimi reached under the seat and found the kit as he said, and his bag held the sewing threads and needles. She went back to the leg and did the best she could with what little she had to work with. "I don't have anything for the pain you will feel", she said but the gunman pulled out a bottle of gin from his coat pocket took a deep pull and handed the bottle to her to use to sterilize the needle. She could fell the warm blood running over her fingers as the outside cold was blowing in the door and the broken windshield.

Snow was blowing in and she started filling rubber gloves from the kit with snow and pressing it into the leg knowing full well it would help in slowing the bleeding.

Night fall was at hand, the bus lights were off as the engine was not running and there was no power to the lights. Temps outside were falling fast and now it looked hopeless for everyone. The gunman had Mimi pack bandages around his leg so he could move up to the roadway and flag down a car.

Johnny still in pain was pushing himself in the dark toward the front of the bus as the gunman worked his way to the highway to flag down help. Johnny reached into a bin that held tools and pulled out emergency flares and was leaving the bus when Mimi called to him,

"Stop he is out of control and thinks nothing about killing"

Johnny felt the warm wet blood flowing from under the bandage and knew he must stop this man, somehow before someone else gets shot or killed.

"You stay put, and I will do what needs to be done get those people untied and help the injured" then he was lost in the snowstorm and darkness.

With nothing but two flares and a pocket knife he was in pursuit of a madman. It was dark the moon was hidden behind clouds and snow falling but he could hear the moans of the gunman as he was working his way back to the roadway.

Johnny reached in his jacket and took out an apple he had saved from his lunch and tossed it in the direction he thought the gunman might be. It must have been close for he fired several times into the darkness.

This allowed Johnny to get a fix on the direction of travel and then there was a blast from a horn, not the bus horn, but the horn that Larry Oaks had.

More shots rang out but, the horn was in another spot and more shots.

Good boy, thought Johnny as he was closing in on the area of the gunman.

The horn blasted again from another direction and more shots were fired into the darkness. It was then that Johnny saw the gunman on his knees reloading his gun. With all his might Johnny ran lighting a flare and blinding the gunman as he fell on him. His gun skidded away lost in the snow.

The two men were both bleeding and loosing fast to their injuries when Larry Oaks made his way to the spot. Johnny handed him the last flare and told him to light it so someone from the road might see.

It was a car of Christmas Travelers that saw the light and a little boy inside shouted "It is the star of Bethlehem as they stopped". A soldier and his family were the travelers and a call was made and soon the police arrived with help to take the injured for care.

The gunman died; his stolen money covered in his own blood before he got to the hospital.

Johnny was in bad shape and the next few hours would tell his fate. Then also the Kicks in the head had Larry in the hospital with a concussion. There were others from the bus that night that had suffered broken arms, cuts and problems. The chatty lady too was being cared for but somehow was a bit speechless in the wake of it all.

Mimi was taken to the police station to give an account for the records. She would not allow any pictures of herself to be taken by the news media. The blood that covered her was mixed with tears and she wanted to go to the aid of those in the hospital.

The next day Mimi was allowed to visit, and Johnny was still out of it and could have no visitors at the time of her arrival. She first went to Larry and he was awake with two very black eyes and a smile when she entered his room. "Take it easy there Gabriel" she said, bringing his trumpet with her.

He asked about Johnny and the others, but as yet they had no word on Johnny, Mrs. Gibson the Chatty lady, was doing well and had regained her voice.

The others were now released to go home for Christmas with lesser injuries.

"You did good Mimi, you held yourself in check for everyone, and now you too should go home and celebrate Christmas with your family".

"Oh, she said, it is here and today I need to be, I must be here for Johnny and I must be here for you, my new friend, and I must share the day with those of us that were so close to being lost in the night, the most holy night of the year."

She reached over and kissed his cheek, and he said, "I never thought I would be kissed by and Angel on Christmas, but darn if it hasn't just happened to me".

A nurse came in and asked Mimi her name and she told the nurse her name and she said there is a man asking to see you and it seems he has a lot to say.

"Is it Johnny the bus driver"? "Yes, he is awake now and will recover from the injury and he said it was you that saved his life." "I just did my best and it was he that tried to save us all".

Mimi made her way to where Johnny was and she was so happy, she came close and kissed his cheek, and strange as it was, Johnny said, "I never thought I would be kissed by an Angel on Christmas, but darn if it hasn't just happened to me". She smiled at him and said there are fresh flowers on your wife's resting place, and a card from you, I signed by proxy.

Tears fell from his eyes of thanks and he could hear music, soft music of Christmas coming from somewhere, He heard the bells on Christmas day, and fell asleep dreaming.

The paper reported the story and it was one strange ending as the girl Mimi could not be found, her job was vacant, and she was never seen thereafter.

It was no strange thing to Johnny or Larry; they had been kissed by an Angel

Somewhere out there, Angels are waiting to help, waiting to serve and if you listen, really listen on Christmas Eve, you will hear them singing on high.

The End

If I could pull the ropes that ring the Bells of Christmas

If I could pull the ropes that ring the Bells of Christmas

I would pull as hard as I could

I would want them to ring so you could hear

I would want the world to hear

I would want God in Heaven to hear

If I could pull the ropes that ring the Bells of Christmas

I would want peace to be for all

I would want health to be yours

Mike Kelley

I would want your life filled with joy

I would want you filled with hope

If I could pull the ropes that ring the Bells of Christmas

I would want for nothing more

A Christmas Trilogy

The Christmas Ride

The Christmas Ride

"Go, Moka, run like the wind" she called to her horse as they left the canyon floor and up to the foothills. Snow falling and out here you could get into trouble fast if you didn't stay on the move. Ruth Morgan was aware of the weather and knew also she was headed to the high country at the wrong time. She had little with her on this trip her horse Moka, a horse she won in a card game with some Native Americans and a mean Canadian trapper who thought he won till she laid out a straight flush against his three kings. In rage he turned the table over and reached out to grab her, but Ruth put a knife through part of his hand so quick that he released her as she took her money from the table, and said "Don't ever try to touch me again for the next time you won't walk away with just a bleeding hand, and you better get to

the doc I haven't cleaned my knife since I skinned a half sick wolf", then she smiled a wicked smile and went out to ride away on Moka, one of the best horses in the area.
Her trip to the ranch would be her last as the bank had taking it back and she just couldn't change things, even with the quick win at cards a few hundred dollars and a horse would not be enough. The time had run out and she needed to be gone. She took her saddle, and bags, a Winchester rifle, some loose gear, her lady slasher, a knife she made herself, and a very few rations, and her Momma's bible. Then on to the trail headed east towards Kentucky which was too many miles away.
The Canadian Trapper would be in chase she knew, but he had a full pack horse and she knew she had a good runner in Moka. She reached the second set of foothills as the snow picked up and she also knew she had another gamble to win, this time with the weather, she would ride up to a spot that few knew of a hidden cabin once used by hunters, but that was in the old days, today the game is further north and the cabin is hidden inside a thick group of pines. This would be her hold over, but she had to move fast to get there before darkness set in.

"Go Moka", she screamed, as the wind picked up and the sky darkened with more snow falling. She was about to turn into the right fork which now was hidden with snow when she heard the call of a voice from somewhere, "Who the heck will be out here in this storm" she ejected and slowed. Looking over the slope she saw a man down and his horse on top of him he was trapped under his own horse that couldn't move.
"Hold on she called out, I'll throw you a rope and pull you free". And with that she tossed a line down to the man as he shifted awaiting the tug to help himself get free. Ruth lashed the line to the saddle horn and hoped it wouldn't break and had Moka walk the line slowly pulling him free. She pulled him up to the trail, but it was clear his leg was broken, the horse was dying of injuries and now it was almost dark.
"I'll have to make a drag for you to get you to a doctor are you able to handle that" she said, but the pain and the exposure to the elements had taken him out for now. She made a drag from branches and laced it together then rolled the big man onto the drag. He was still out as she went down the hill to where the horse lay, as the horse was bleeding and as wolves had

attacked the animal which would die soon she shot the horse. Then she removed the saddle and his saddle bags and his rifle and returned to the man and the drag which she hitched to Moka and rode up the hill to get off the lower pass. She didn't like this as it felt like she was carving out a path for the Trapper to follow, but she couldn't just leave him there.
Moka, pulled the drag along over the mountain trial with the help of some soft snow and up to where the rocks stopped their progress. They now had to release the drag and somehow get the man over the saddle of the horse sideways to move over the rocks and into the thick pines. Again, the rope was used this time to tie to the midsection of the man and over a tree limb to lift him into place. This would cause a lot of pain but as he was already past that point, she secured the leg with a branch removed from the drag and tied it to keep his leg from moving and laced his two legs together. He looked like a mummy, but it worked, and he was laid over the back of Moka, Ruth walked her horse up and around the trees and rocks a quarter of a mile more and to the cabin.
As they arrived at the cabin it was now dark and snow falling at a fast rate. Ruth moved Moka to the door sideways to release the man,

as he slid to the floor just at the entry of the cabin he screamed out with pain, his eyes closed tight as she pulled and tugged to make him a mat on the floor unable to move him more. Then she secured Moka and gave her oats she had packed for her and tied her behind the cabin. She then pulled the injured man's saddle into the cabin to use as a support for his head as she would attempt to set the leg. His saddle bag was heavy and fell to the wood floor with a clunk. Now she started a fire to warm the cabin it wouldn't take much as it was one room maybe twelve feet by twelve. Once the fire was going and the room was warm, she cut away the seam in his pants that run up the leg and exposed the broken leg that needed to be set. The break was at a right angle to the body so she would have to pull in that direction and then center the broken bone over the break to set it straight. It would take everything she had to do this and again she used the rope tied around his foot and then around the door latch and her own midsection. She would lean away from the rope to tighten it and then at the last second, she would jump pulling the rope tight and hopefully the leg back in place. His eyes were still closed, and she counted to three to no one but herself and on three she pulled with a great snapping sound that came from the rope and a scream from the man, but it worked, the leg was back together and looked to be straight. His leg was greatly swollen, and she could tell that at least it had a chance to heal. Ruth untied herself and sat on the floor beside the man. It took all she had to deal with this and at a time she would have chosen otherwise.

Then she spoke out looking at the man, "You darn fool, this is not the time or place to get hurt you know, what are you doing out here anyway, don't you know it is dangerous and your horse stepped in a hole hidden in the snow deep enough to launch you both down the slope, you're lucky to be alive". The man lay there without a word, he was out to the world. It was late and the snow would hold off any forward movement of the trapper, so she undid her bed roll and lay down to rest. Out in the wild you rest lightly always listening for sounds, this could mean your life or death at times. Ruth lay listening and now the man's breathing had fallen into a rhythm softly as she closed her eyes.

This lasted for a few hours till she awoke to the sound of Moka pacing and then the call, Ruth set up and listened as she got up to check on Moka, she picked up her Winchester and opened the door to realize she was face to face with a black bear that with one swipe had launched her rifle across the cabin. Then the bear rushed her and pulled her arm towards him but she with her free hand whipped out the lady slasher and cut into the bear, but it pulled at her and with a crash of it's huge paw it cut into her back ripping at her skin, and again she cut into the bear this time more deeply and again. It was bleeding but still on the attack when the sound came, and the bear fell. The big man had pulled his saddle bag open took out a pistol and fired shooting the bear. The cabin had a smell of gunpowder, blood and smoke, but she was alive, and the bear moaned trying to leave but fell to the snow just outside the cabin door and moved no more.

Ruth looked into the eyes of the man and for the first time she saw his blue glow by the fire light and she spoke, "You saved my life, I was about to be killed and you saved me" then she slumped to the floor with her own blood mixed with that of the bear and cried.

The stranger now spoke, "Come closer and let me help stop that bleeding take a cloth from my saddlebag and let me make a bandage and there is a bottle I keep for cuts, take that and allow me to wash over the cuts the bear made it will sting, but it will help keep away infection". She sat and looked him in the eyes and said, "Look at you, playing doctor with your own leg broken", then they both laughed through their shared pain.

"My name is Luke and I was out here running down a man I have a warrant for, his name is Louis Preston a trapper from Candia, I am a US Marshall and was headed to Stockton in search for him when my horse tripped and tumbled down the hill and came down on top of me".

"Well Marshal Luke, my name is Ruth, and you may not have to go to Stockton as I just came from there and the trapper your looking for is heading this way".

Luke took this time to rip up the cloth into a bandage, then poured alcohol over the cuts as Ruth displayed her back to him. There were several deep gashes in her flesh and now with the bandages in place the bleeding slowed.

"Look at us, you broken up, me cut up, together we don't even make one good person" Ruth laughed as she covered herself with her last shirt from her saddle bag.

"Your trapper will be coming this way he wants my horse and my money I won in a card game, he had a good hand, but I drew into a

straight flush and left him with a hole in his hand bleeding a lot worse than me".
Luke looked into her eyes, they were a soft green that shown lovely against her red hair, "You are messing with a man that has a record of killing more than wild game, albeit you might be a bit wilder than he expected".
"Oh, I have my moments but all in all I choose my battles and don't go looking for trouble, after all the world is full of Marshals without broken legs that might give chase", then she laughed again.
Luke thanked her for all she had done for him, then they traded a few words and lay to rest as they were sure the trapper would be held up by the storm as now it was well over a foot deep and still falling.
"Good Night, Lady Ruth, sleep well he said", but Ruth was already asleep resting just a few feet from the Marshall.
Morning came with the sound of gunfire down the hill, it awoke them both with a quick awareness of the next battle to fight.
Ruth sat up and said "good morning sounds like your man is on the way", then stepped out in door to check things out, the bear that was cut and shot was not there just a trail of blood as he must have had more in him then was

thought. He had moved away and just may have been the reason for the sound of gunfire down the hill.

Ruth then strung her trusty rope between two trees down on the trail leading to the cabin, it was low in the snow but high enough to trip up a horse and allow them time to be ready to take down the trapper.

She returned to the cabin and Luke had pulled himself up on a stool by the window and was holding his rifle at the ready should it be his man coming.

Ruth told of the snare she had set and put more wood on the fire. "The winds will hold the smoke to let him know I am here, and he will think me stupid enough to allow him to sneak up".

"Good, this will work out a bit better as it would be hard to run him down with a broken leg, and just sitting is a bit painful but I have a clear view to the trail".

Ruth, didn't say a word she took to her bag and pulled out some coffee beans and filled the pot with snow and sat it over the fire to melt as she broke the beans into a powder with the butt end of her Winchester, the fresh smell welcomed them to a new day.

Luke turned to her and spoke, "I don't suppose you have any eggs and bacon in that bag of yours do you", she turned and said "no just a few stale biscuits and some honey is the best you'll get this morning" and she placed the cold biscuits near the fire to warm as the coffee was lifting a fragrance of the Gods around the little cabin.

As they ate and made themselves ready down the hill was the trapper Louis Preston, a man mad at the world, mean with a dark spirit. He shot and killed a bear, but then he realized it had been wounded by someone else and he thought he knew who. "That woman and her knife, she will get hers before this day is out, and that horse will be mine, and all the money too. I might just have to tie her down first, slap her around a bit, and run my knife through her hand, then as she screams, I'll laugh in her face as I shoot her eyes out".

He did smell the wood smoke and tied his pack horse to a tree and moved on foot up through the pines towards the cabin. Under the pines the snow was light, and he walked quickly towards the smell of wood smoke till he came on sight of the cabin. He then laid down like the snake he was and crawled forward allowing

the falling snow to cover him using nature to help in his quest.
Luke watching the trail was unaware of the man under the snow inching his way forward as he enjoyed the warm biscuits with coffee, it was also Ruth that was making herself ready to greet the trapper when outside they heard the sound of the horse stirring behind the cabin and without warning there he was, the trapper had mounted the horse and rode around the cabin at full gallop laughing that the horse is now his and ran down the trail.
Snow was flying from the feet as Moka, as she was being whipped running down the trail, but right into the snare Ruth had sat and when they hit the snare they both went down, the trapper tumbled off and into the trees beside the trail hitting his head and Moka lay there for a second then up righted herself and walked back towards the cabin. The Marshall tried to stand, but Ruth told him to sit she would bring the trapper back. Then with a rifle in hand she moved down and saw the trapper lying face down in the snow and approached slowly as he spun around and grabbed at her feet the rifle fell as she too went down at the grip then came a smack across her face as he sat up and held her down. She had her knife, but it was in her

boot and he was holding her arms looking down into her face with a mean sneer he spoke, "Your luck just ran out lady, your mine now, and will feel more pain than I did from that knife of yours, you will die today, and I'll toss your bones to wolves".

He reached inside his coat and took out his revolver and shot her through the hand, blood spraying and as he held her arm down with his knee he pulled her other arm free to shoot it, "I think I will double your pain and repay you well" but before he did another shot was fired the Marshall had raised his rifle and it took to the trappers shoulder sending his gun into the snow and turning the trapper to face him. This was all Ruth needed as her hand now free took her knife and she shoved it into his chest as he rolled off her exchanging blood. Still alive he was spitting out blood trying to curse her and the Marshall, but it was useless, and his life ended.

Ruth, felt the burn through her hand and stood with her blood dripping as she made her way back to Luke who was using his rifle as a crutch and he told her to go to the cabin and tie off the wound he would be there as soon as he could make it. The snow was colored red with blood but again she was alive and again the Marshall had saved her.

When Luke made it back inside the cabin Ruth was laying on the floor the hand still bleeding, and she was as white as a ghost. He spoke to her, but she was out of it and he cleaned the hand and tied a bandage around it, but the blood was leaking through he held her hand and pulled it to himself putting pressure to slow the bleeding. He sat bent over her and he himself fell asleep.

Ruth awoke dazed by the loss of blood and found her hand in the hand of Luke who lay over it with his body, she knew he was putting pressure on the hand to stop the bleeding. She has no feeling in the hand, but her heart was warmed by his actions. She freed herself from him as he lay asleep his leg, she noticed, was badly swollen and now turning a deep purple color.

The movements he had made to bring down Louis Preston had hindered his recovery and now she feared he might even loose the leg if he didn't get help soon. She had to return to Stockton for medical help as the Marshall could not make the ride.

When Luke awoke, he was running a fever, and this was another sign he needed help now. Ruth spoke to him with her plan, "Marshall, I am going to ride back to Stockton and get help for you I'll take the body of Preston to town and the packhorse, I have removed some food items from the packhorse. You will be ok for now just stay off the leg till I come back. The weather is not good so don't worry if it takes a few days. I will be back by Christmas and we will celebrate being alive".

Luke was not about to go anywhere; he was weak and worn and the fever was keeping him even more planted. Ruth had left everything at an arms-reach for him and stooped and kissed his cheek and again said "I'll be back for Christmas" and closed the door.

Moka, had fallen but was unhurt and this was some good luck, Ruth put Louis Preston over the back of the packhorse and attached a line to it as she and Moka, headed back to Stockton. Her hand hurt and she felt she might lose some use of it but that was to deal with when that time might come. The snow was blinding and somehow, they made it to the canyon and into Stockton.

The sheriff was given a quick report about Preston and the Marshall and given the packhorse and guns to cover whatever expenses might be to plant his dark sole.

Then she went to the doctor to report the injury of the Marshall, but the doctor took quick notice of her hand. Then she went on and reported the cuts to her back from the bear. He treated them all and sewed up the open cuts and rebandaged them. Her hand he said will not heal fully it will lose the motion of two fingers, but it should otherwise heal up. He wanted to give her something for the pain, but she would not take it as she wanted to be alert for the ride back to the cabin.

The Doctor could not make the trip himself, he had his hands full in town with several others, however; his son was working with him and he told his son the issue and he was to ride out and give aid to the Marshall and with that he mounted up and rode on out of town that evening. Ruth remained till morning to have the hand looked at and treated one more time. The doctor's wife had fashioned a glove to cover the hand to help in the healing. Her back was treated and covered with new bandages and although she was sore and a bit beat-up, she rode out the next morning, Christmas Eve, she had to make it back to the cabin.

The snow had stopped, and the winds were mild, so she was making good time. As she rode into the foothills, she was passed by the doctor's son returning from the cabin they talked for a few minutes and he reported the Marshall will be OK to travel just after New-Years and that he was in good spirits. Ruth thanked him and paid for the care given with the money she won in the card game and moved over the second foot hill as night was falling. "It won't be long now Moka, we will celebrate this Christmas in a cabin, we will celebrate".

It was fully dark as she rode up to the cabin, the sky had cleared, and the air was fresh it had a special feel to it. The windows were glowing with candles it looked so inviting, then as she stepped inside, she was so surprised to see a tree decorated and the fire glowing and a cooked ham on the table. "Merry Christmas" shouted Luke as she came in from the cold. "How did you do this and where did the ham come from" and then she saw candies on the tree and a stocking hanging over the fireplace, "how can this be"?

"Santa did it" Luke laughed, "really it was the Doctor and his Wife and Son"

"Oh, I am so happy about this it makes me want to cry", then the tears came as Ruth sat to take it all in.

The Doctors son, Seth said that his Mother had picked up on what happened here, and she felt we had gotten a bit close in the exchange from the words you spoke while making sure I was getting help, and that she wanted us to be able to celebrate this Christmas as a couple".

Ruth, looked at Luke and he was now lashed in with wrapping around his leg and a cane to walk with, "Oh what wonderful people to have done this, and they don't even know us, they have an image of us that I must have projected from my worries about you".

She sat down beside him and the fire had a glow that lit the room and with the candles in the windows it was as if they were in a special place on this special night and there was Christmas magic in the air.

Then they looked out to the night the clear sky shown all the stars around as the moonlight was cast over the snow. This was Christmas. They shared the night with a warmth given, Ruth read from the bible her mother had given her the story of the Christ child and then they could almost hear the angles singing, "Go tell it on the Mountain".

That was their first Christmas together. But somewhere in Kentucky down in some back woods cabin you might see the windows with

candles, and hear children singing as by the fire side sits an old man with a limp, and a woman with a scared hand and a warm feeling of Christmas being shared as a hand me down bible tells it's story, and children with their noses pressed against the windows not to see Santa, but to listen for the Angels singing, "Go Tell it on the Mountain".
This was the Christmas Ride.
The End

Mike Kelley

Will We Be Thinking of Him?

Will we be thinking of him?

There is a time to remember
Oh, so long ago
A star was brightly shining
Bringing light to the world below
Shepherds heard angels singing
And went to a holy place
There they found a baby
And looked into Jesus face
The world received a Savior
A gift from God above
What have we done this Christmas?
To remember this special love?

Will we be thinking of him?
With our packages and bows
Or will it be colored lights
Or maybe our new clothes
Will we be thinking of him?
With a wreath on our door
Or will it be a tree
Or maybe something more

Mike Kelley

I choose to remember in my special way
Reading from my bible
What happened on that day
To love the world around me
I know that is what he would do
And thank Our Father in Heaven
For the gift he gave
For me and you

A Christmas Trilogy

Grandma's Bible

Grandma's Bible

Once I looked through my Grandma's bible as
a child and was amazed at what I found.
There were pressed between the pages
treasures she kept close to her heart and in her
own way close to God.
There were flowers pressed to the pages of a
special event of joy and flowers from the
passing of loved ones.
There were newspaper clips of history
changing and an anniversary card from
Grandpa signed with love,
There were notes written from verse to verse
and a letter or two from family away
There were lines underlined in color with
special dates written in.
There were pictures of the life of Christ and a
cross made of lace.
There were pages worn in her bible some
stained with tears of hurt and tears of joy.

There were so many things to see but the one that meant the most to me came on Christmas Eve.

It was a cold winter in Kentucky and our old coal stoves bottom had just burned out, so we went to our Grandparents house till a new heat stove could be installed.

It was just a few days before Christmas and this made things extra special for me as a child. It was on this visit that I found Grandma's Bible on a table beside the chair she always sat and the treasures within.

Grandma smiled and called my name when she saw me looking through the pages, and came and sit down with me and without a word turned the pages to the second chapter of Luke and began to read to me.

Her voice had such a loving feel as she read the words and through her eyes that Christmas Eve I saw Mary and Joseph and could almost hear the donkeys feet on the journey to Bethlehem. There was a great crowd of people and no place to stay in that city.

 Mary was soon to be the mother of Jesus and with Joseph they came upon a stable to rest. I listened as Grandma told the story as if she had been there herself. I could smell the hay and see all the animals around.

A Christmas Trilogy

Grandma's face was aglow while telling of Jesus and his birth. She made me to understand as she moved my fingers over the lines that there was a great star, shepherds, and angles. With her voice I heard "Glory to God in the Highest and on earth peace and goodwill to men".

Then after reading with arms around me I was made to understand why Jesus was born and tears fell from her eyes while speaking, (all treasures have a price).

She closed her bible and placed her hand over mine on top of that holy book, closed her eyes and bowed her head and spoke to God with me in her lap.

I have lived a lifetime since that Christmas Eve but never have I forgotten.

I guess if I think back to that time, we would be considered poor but I, well I, found a real treasure in Grandma's bible.

Mike Kelley

A Christmas Trilogy

NOEL

N, Nestled in the joy of this season

O, Oh, sing the songs of gold

E, Enjoy the folks around you

L, Love them all, young and old

May you find peace and love and the true gift of Christmas.
                    Mike Kelley

www.ingramcontent.com/pod-product-compliance
Lightning Source LLC
Chambersburg PA
CBHW070049230426
43661CB00005B/835